6/14

Lexile: _____

AR/BL: _____

AR Points: _____

## NOTE TO PARENTS

Welcome to Kingfisher Readers! This program is designed to help young readers build skills, confidence, and a love of reading as they explore their favorite topics.

These tips can help you get more from the experience of reading books together. But remember, the most important thing is to make reading fun!

*Tips to Warm Up Before Reading*

- Look through the book with your child. Ask them what they notice about the pictures.
- Wonder aloud together. Ask questions and make predictions. What will this book be about? What are some words we could expect to find on these pages?

*While Reading*

- Take turns or read together until your child takes over.
- Point to the words as you say them.
- When your child gets stuck on a word, ask if the picture could help. Then think about the first letter too.
- Accept and praise your child's contributions.

*After Reading*

- Look back at the things your child found interesting. Encourage connections to other things you both know.
- Draw pictures or make models to explore these ideas.
- Read the book again soon, to build fluency.

With five distinct levels and a wealth of appealing topics, the Kingfisher Readers series provides children with an exciting way to learn to read about the world around them. Enjoy!

Ellie Costa, M.S. Ed.
*Literacy Specialist, Bank Street School for Children, New York*

**KINGFISHER**
LONDON & NEW YORK

Copyright © Kingfisher 2014
Published in the United States by Kingfisher,
175 Fifth Ave., New York, NY 10010
Kingfisher is an imprint of Macmillan Children's Books, London.
All rights reserved.

Distributed in the U.S. and Canada by Macmillan,
175 Fifth Ave., New York, NY 10010

Library of Congress Cataloging-in-Publication data
has been applied for.

Series editor: Thea Feldman
Literacy consultant: Ellie Costa, Bank Street School for Children, New York

ISBN: 978-0-7534-7146-3 (HB)
ISBN: 978-0-7534-7147-0 (PB)

Kingfisher books are available for special promotions
and premiums. For details contact: Special Markets
Department, Macmillan, 175 Fifth Ave., New York, NY 10010.

For more information, please visit
www.kingfisherbooks.com

Printed in China
9 8 7 6 5 4 3 2 1
1TR/0314/WKT/UG/105MA

Picture credits
The Publisher would like to thank the following for permission to reproduce their material.
Every care has been taken to trace copyright holders. However, if there have been unintentional
omissions or failure to trace copyright holders, we apologize and will, if informed, endeavor
to make corrections in any future edition.
Top = t; Bottom = b; Center = c; Left = l; Right = r
Cover Shutterstock/Johan Swanepoel/Paul Paladin; Pages 4l Shutterstock/Elena Schweitzer; 4r Shutterstock/
Elenamiv; 5 Science Photo Library/David Nunuk; 6 Shutterstock/PaulPaladin; 7t&b Shutterstock/sebikus;
8–9 KF Archive; 10 Shutterstock/liseykina; 11t Shutterstock/Cristian Zamfir; 11b Shutterstock/tadamichi;
12 Shutterstock/USBFCO; 13 KF Archive; 14 Shutterstock/Richard Schramm; 15 KF Archive; 16 Shutterstock/
Kirschner; 17 Shutterstock/MarcelClemens; 18–19 Shutterstock/PavleMarjanovic; 20 Shutterstock/G. K.;
21 Science Photo Library/Andrzej Wojcicki; 22 KF Archive; 23 KF Archive; 24–25 KF Archive; 26 Science Photo
Library/Julian Baum; 27 Science Photo Library/Mark Garlick; 28t Corbis/ClassicStock/H. Armstrong;
28b KF Archive; 29 KF Archive; 30t KF Archive; 30b KF Archive; 31 KF Archive.

# KINGFISHER
# READERS

level
2

# Sun, Moon, and Stars

Hannah Wilson

## KINGFISHER
### NEW YORK

# Contents

# Up in the sky

The Sun shines every day.

At night you can see the Moon.

You might be able to see
some stars at night, too.

Let's find out all about
the Sun, Moon, and stars!

# A sense of size

The Sun is millions of miles from Earth, but we can see it because it is so big.

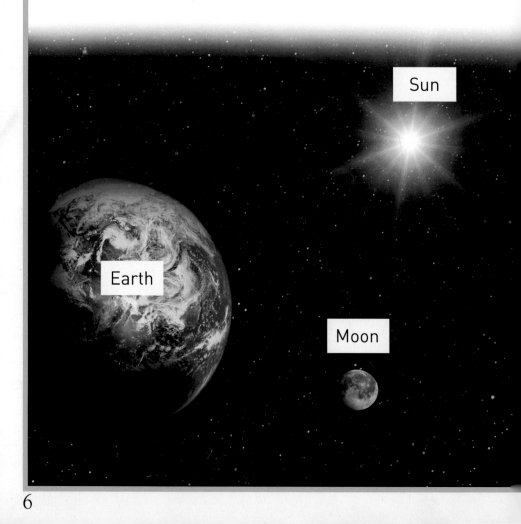

Sun

Earth

Moon

One million Earths could fit inside the Sun!

The Moon is smaller than Earth—50 Moons could fit inside Earth!

# A giant star

The Sun is a giant star in **space**.

**Gas** inside a star is so hot,
it makes the star glow!

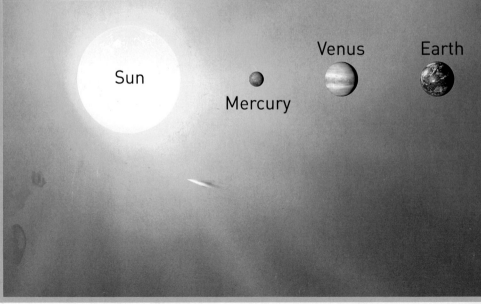

Sun

Mercury

Venus

Earth

Earth is a **planet**.

Eight planets travel around the Sun.

Mars

Jupiter

Saturn

Uranus

Neptune

# Super sunlight

The Sun is so hot and bright that it heats and lights Earth, even though it is so far away.

Sunlight is full of **energy**.

Some living things use that energy.

The Sun's energy warms this lizard
so it can move around.

Plants use
the Sun's
energy
to make
their own
food.

# Day and night

Earth travels around the Sun.

At the same time, Earth spins on an imaginary stick called an axis.

When one side of Earth turns to the Sun, it has daytime.

The other side has night.

Sun

Earth never stops spinning,
so each side has day and night
over and over again.

It takes one day and night for Earth
to turn all the way around on its axis.

It takes a year for Earth to travel
all the way around the Sun.

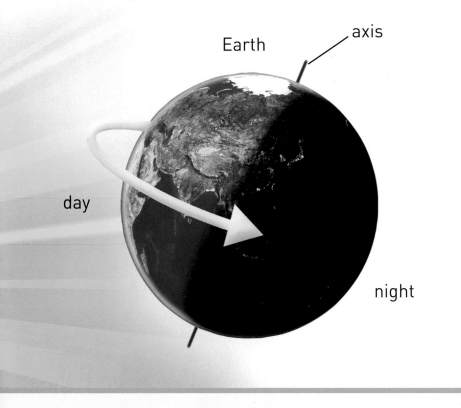

Earth

axis

day

night

# Changing seasons

spring                    summer

fall                    winter

Earth's axis tilts a little
as it moves around the Sun.

So different parts of Earth
are tilted closer to to the Sun
at different times of the year.

The parts that tilt toward the Sun
have summer, and the parts
that tilt away have winter.

summer

winter

# Moons

Moons travel around planets.

Some planets do not have moons.

Jupiter has more than 60 moons!

Jupiter

moons

Earth has one moon.

It has no air and is dry and rocky.

# Light of the Moon

The Moon shines at night because light from the Sun **reflects** off it.

crescent moon

full moon

The Moon does not make
its own light.

Instead, the Sun lights up
different parts of the Moon
as the Moon travels around Earth.

The Moon looks like it changes
shape, but we can only see the parts
that are lit by the Sun.

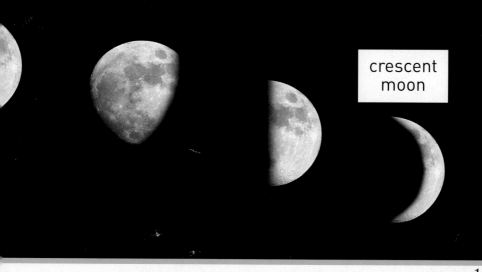

crescent
moon

# On the surface

plains

mountains

There are **plains** and mountains on the Moon's surface.

The surface has many circles too.

The circles are called craters.

Craters are dents from giant rocks that crashed into the Moon!

crater

# To the Moon

In 1969, **astronauts** landed
on the Moon for the first time.

They left footprints on the surface
that will be there forever,
because the Moon has
no wind or rain or anything else
that could destroy them!

# Billions of stars

If you look up at the sky
on a clear night, you might
see a cloudy white stripe.

The stripe is the Milky Way galaxy.

A galaxy has billions of stars and their planets and moons.

We are part of the Milky Way galaxy.

# Star colors

Stars can be different sizes and colors.

Some are red and called red dwarves.

They are smaller and cooler
than our Sun.

Some are blue and are much hotter
and bigger than our Sun.

They are called blue giants.

# Seeing far away

People use **telescopes** to see stars, moons, and planets, because they are so far away.

Huge telescopes can be on remote islands or even out in space.

The Hubble Space Telescope circles
Earth once every 97 minutes
and uses energy from the Sun!

# Star patterns

Imagine drawing lines between stars as if you were connecting dots to make a picture.

A group of stars that form a picture is called a constellation.

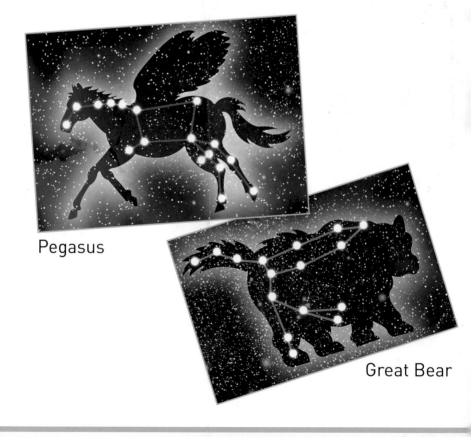

Pegasus

Great Bear

Can you find the Great Bear
and Pegasus on this map
of the constellations?

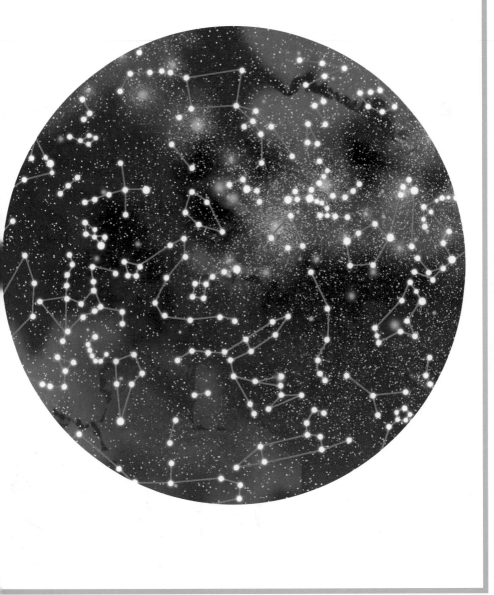

# Glossary

**astronaut** a person who travels in space

**energy** the power needed to do an activity, such as moving or growing

**galaxy** a very large group of billions of stars, along with their planets and moons

**gas** something in the air you cannot see

**plain** a large, flat area of land

**planet** a large, round object that travels around a star

**reflect** to hit and bounce back off something, such as sunlight off the Moon

**space** the place beyond Earth's sky

**telescope** an instrument that shows distant objects up close

If you have enjoyed reading
this book, look out for more in
the Kingfisher Readers series!

**Collect
and read
them all!**

For a full list of Kingfisher Readers books, plus
guidance for teachers and parents and activities
and fun stuff for kids, go to the Kingfisher Readers
website: **www.kingfisherreaders.com**